To *Baby Anthony*

With love
from *Aunt Barb & Uncle Lou*

Date *11-12-16*

Children are a gift from God.

Little Boys

Boys

Are
Wonderfully
Made

HARVEST HOUSE PUBLISHERS
EUGENE, OREGON

Little Boys Are Wonderfully Made

Copyright © 2016 by Harvest House Publishers

Published by Harvest House Publishers
Eugene, Oregon 97402
www.harvesthousepublishers.com

ISBN 978-0-7369-6584-2

Design and production by Dugan Design Group, Bloomington, Minnesota

Harvest House Publishers has made every effort to trace the ownership of all poems and quotes. In the event of a question arising from the use of a poem or quote, we regret any error made and will be pleased to make the necessary correction in future editions of this book.

Photos: Fotolia—pages 1,6,7,10,14,15,17,25,29,31,33,34,38,42,46,47,48
iStockphoto—pages 19,37
All others by Dugan Design Group.

Scripture quotations are from:

The Living Bible copyright © 1971. Used by permission of Tyndale House Publishers, Inc., Carol Stream, Illinois 60188. All rights reserved.

The Holy Bible, New International Version®, NIV®. Copyright © 1973, 1978, 1984, 2011 by Biblica, Inc.® Used by permission. All rights reserved worldwide.

Printed in China

15 16 17 18 19 20 21 22 23 24 / LP / 10 9 8 7 6 5 4 3 2 1

I praise you because I am fearfully and wonderfully made; your works are wonderful, I know that full well.

THE BOOK OF PSALMS

God Has a PLAN FOR HIM

He's arrived with God's good plan. He was made for a purpose. Will he be the kind of boy to discover his God-given talents early in life and fall easily into step, or will he be one to try his hand at many ventures to determine what fits, what feels right, what thrills his spirit? No matter. God is with him. You too. Always will be.

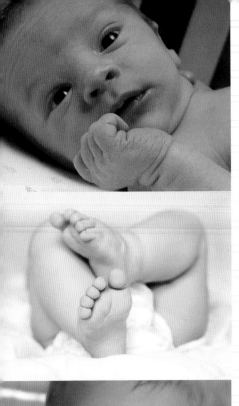

If one feels the need of something grand, something infinite, something that makes one feel aware of God, one need not go far to find it. I think that I see something deeper, more infinite, more eternal than the ocean in the expression of the eyes of a little baby when it wakes in the morning and coos or laughs because it sees the sun shining on its cradle.

VINCENT VAN GOGH

Joy delights in joy.

WILLIAM SHAKESPEARE

Lord,
please bless this
little one with a
happy heart.

He's a BLESSING

Here he is! At last. His healthy cry has captured your heart already. Bundle him up, rock him long into the night, and tenderly tuck him in. Do it all again just because you can. It's hard to get enough of him, isn't it? Truly he is wonderfully made! He is a beautiful, little-boy blessing.

> Those blessings are sweetest that are won with prayer and worn with thanks.
>
> THOMAS GOODWIN

What are little boys made of, made of;
What are little boys made of?
"Snaps and snails, and puppy-dogs' tails;
And that's what little boys are made of, made of."

TRADITIONAL NURSERY RHYME, EARLY NINETEENTH CENTURY

Every child born into the world
is a new thought of God, an ever fresh and
radiant possibility.

KATE DOUGLAS WIGGIN

"For I know the plans I have for you," says the Lord. "They are plans for good and not for evil, to give you a future and a hope."

THE BOOK OF JEREMIAH

Keep true to the dreams of thy youth.

FRIEDRICH VON SCHILLER

To accomplish great things, we must not only act, but also dream; not only plan, but also believe.

ANATOLE FRANCE

He Makes the World DIFFERENT

His birth changes the world a little bit, your world a lot. The gentle sound of his quiet breathing seems to bring heaven to earth. And his touch, now soft and exploring, will soon enough grow strong, able to make a difference. Pray he learns early and well to choose good, to find ways to be a light. Forever choosing to side with love.

A child's tear rends the heavens.

YIDDISH PROVERB

Lord,
please bless
this little one with
strength to grow.

Blessed be childhood, which brings down something of heaven into the midst of our rough earthliness.

HENRI FREDERIC AMIEL

First we had each other.
Then we had you.
Now we have everything.

AUTHOR UNKNOWN

Our days are a kaleidoscope. Every instant a change takes place in the contents. New harmonies, new contrasts, new combinations of every sort. Nothing ever happens twice alike.

HENRY WARD BEECHER

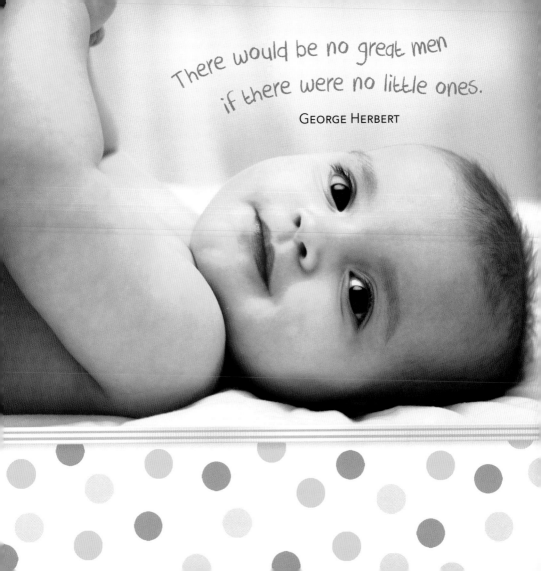

There would be no great men
if there were no little ones.

GEORGE HERBERT

He Is a TREASURE

He is amazing! Unique. Rare. A darling if there ever was one. No one else in the whole wide world is like him! He was created from nothing to something by the very hand of God. And so hold him close. Even when he's grown and on his own, stay close in spirit and whisper, "You are such a treasure."

Lord,
please bless this
little one with hugs
and kisses and smiling
faces.

When our babe he goeth walking in his garden,
Around his tinkling feet the sunbeams play;
The posies they are good to him,
And bow them as they should to him,
As fareth he upon his kingly way;
And birdlings of the wood to him
Make music, gentle music, all the day,
When our babe he goeth walking in his garden.

EUGENE FIELD, *GARDEN AND CRADLE*

Ordinary riches can be stolen, real riches cannot. In your soul are infinitely precious things that cannot be taken from you.

OSCAR WILDE

Children are the hands by which we take hold of heaven.

HENRY WARD BEECHER

hildren that makes the heart too big for the body.

RALPH WALDO EMERSON

The Best FOR HIM

G od placed him in your arms to love to the ends of the earth, help along the way, and protect until he can do that for himself. With God you are capable of doing your very best for him. He is worth all your efforts, all your strength, and all your love. Tell him often that of all the things he will come to learn, this one thing is certain: he can always count on you.

The soul is strong that trusts in goodness.

PHILIP MASSINGER

Lord,
please bless
this little one with
all he needs.

Who is not attracted by bright and pleasant children to prattle, to creep, and to play with them?

EPICTETUS

No language can express the power and beauty and heroism of a mother's love.

EDWIN H. CHAPIN

It is one of the most beautiful facts in this human existence of ours, that we remember the earliest and freshest part of it most vividly. Doubtless it was meant that our childhood should live on in us forever.

LUCY LARCOM

The only gift is a portion of thyself.

RALPH WALDO EMERSON

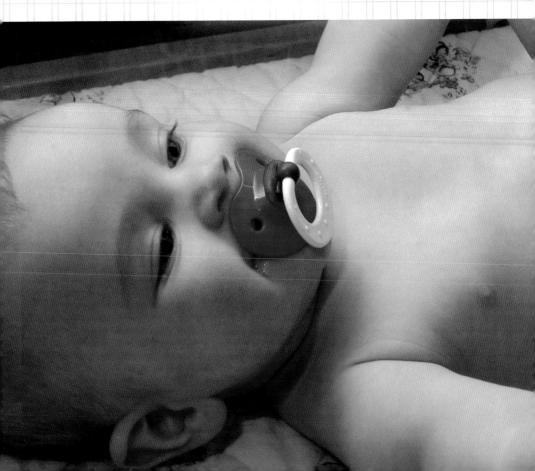

Learning TOGETHER

He is changing and developing so quickly. It's fascinating—inspiring, really. At first he couldn't even find your face, and then suddenly he's looking deeply into your eyes, making sounds that mean something, and working hard to move forward. You too. Try looking a little deeper and learning a bit more because wisdom and truth are good for the soul.

I was like a boy playing on the sea-shore, and diverting myself now and then finding a smoother pebble or a prettier shell than ordinary, whilst the great ocean of truth lay all undiscovered before me.

ISAAC NEWTON

For wisdom and truth will enter the very ce

The best teacher is the one who suggests rather than dogmatizes, and inspires his listener with the wish to teach himself.

EDWARD BULWER-LYTTON

I am not young enough to know everything.

OSCAR WILDE

...er of your being, filling your life with joy.

THE BOOK OF PROVERBS

He Is Full of SURPRISES

Oh, look at him winking and blinking and carrying on. And that smile! Where did *that* come from? He is full of surprises. And as he gives them out, one after another, generously and without a care, he creates an ability in you to love him all the more. Amazing! He's such a charmer!

Our home joys are the most delightful earth affords, and the joy of parents in their children is the most holy joy of humanity.

JOHANN HEINRICH PESTALOZZI

A little child, a limber elf,
   Singing, dancing to itself,
A fairy thing with red round cheeks
   That always finds and never seeks,
Makes such a vision to the sight
   As fills a father's eyes with light.

SAMUEL TAYLOR COLERIDGE

Motherhood: All love begins and ends there.

ROBERT BROWNING

Never fear spoiling children by making them too happy. Happiness is the atmosphere in which all good affections grow.

THOMAS BRAY

Mother is the name for God in the lips and
hearts of little children.

WILLIAM MAKEPEACE THACKERAY

A Promise of PATIENCE

Every day he strains mightily to grow bigger and learn more. And then he does it again the next day and each day after that. So begins his push to become the little boy he was born to be. He tries with all his might. You are his coach, his encourager, his helper. He'll need you to be patient, especially on the days—and nights—he's giving it his all. Practice patience and be his blessing.

The dignity, the grandeur, the tenderness, the everlasting and divine significance of motherhood.

THOMAS DE WITT TALMAGE

Our patience will achieve more than our force.

EDMUND BURKE

Patience is the
companion of wisdom.

SAINT AUGUSTINE

It was the policy of the good old gentleman to
make his children feel that home was the
happiest place in the world; and I value this
delicious home-feeling as one of the choicest
gifts a parent can bestow.

WASHINGTON IRVING

First keep the peace within yourself, then you can also bring peace to others.

THOMAS á KEMPIS

Good TEACHERS

In his lifetime, he will have many teachers. You have the chance to be his very *best* teacher. While he's little, he looks to you for understanding. When he's a wee bit bigger in the britches, he'll look elsewhere and to others for answers to his questions. Pray for wisdom…that he might seek it, you might have it, and others would freely give it.

He who teaches children learns more than they do.

GERMAN PROVERB

Lord,
please bless this
little one with a good
night's sleep.

We need love's tender lessons taught
As only weakness can;
God hath His small interpreters;
The child must teach the man.

JOHN GREENLEAF WHITTIER

For the Lord grants wisdom! His
every word is a treasure of knowledge
and understanding.

THE BOOK OF PROVERBS

A child can ask a thousand
questions that the wisest man cannot answer.

JACOB ABBOTT

IT'S HIS

He's the picture of pure innocence, and he's already captured your heart along with everything else you're made of. Crazy about him? Well, of course! He's amazing and totally worthy of your adoring attention. If he were to ask for the impossible, he'd find you hunting it down for him. Just for him.

Children are the anchors of a mother's life.
SOPHOCLES

To love a child changes everything.
Every. Single. Thing.
ANGELA THOMAS, *52 THINGS SONS NEED FROM THEIR MOMS*

Recommend to your children virtue;
that alone can make them happy,
not gold.
LUDWIG VAN BEETHOVEN

Children have neither past nor future;
they enjoy the present.
JEAN DE LA BRUYERE

The family is the country of the heart.

GIUSEPPE MAZZINI

Prayers FOR HIM

He needs your prayers. As much as you can, as often as you can, as faithfully as you are able. One day he will understand how a simple whisper of hope presented to the faithful Almighty makes everything better—blisters, bruises, and broken hearts included. And he will call you blessed.

A grateful thought toward heaven is of itself a prayer.

GOTTHOLD E. LESSING

Lord,
please bless this
little one with a
loving heart.

I remember
my mother's prayers,
and they have
always followed me.

ABRAHAM LINCOLN

God has two dwellings: one in
heaven, and the other in a meek
and thankful heart.

IZAAK WALTON

Forever and Always

He is able to wrap you around his heart with a smile. He can win you over with a chuckle. May heaven help you when he falls asleep in your arms! What a lucky little boy he is to know you are wholly and totally devoted to him, that you love him forever and always.